Hiking and Camping

Paul Mason

Smart Apple Media

This edition first published in 2008 in the United States of America by Smart Apple Media.
All rights reserved. No part of this book may be reproduced in any form or by any means
without written permission from the publisher.

Smart Apple Media
2140 Howard Drive West
North Mankato, Minnesota 56003

First published in 2007 by
MACMILLAN EDUCATION AUSTRALIA PTY LTD
627 Chapel Street, South Yarra, Australia 3141

Visit our Web site at www.macmillan.com.au or go directly to www.macmillanlibrary.com.au

Associated companies and representatives throughout the world.

Library of Congress Cataloging-in-Publication Data

Mason, Paul, 1967-
    Hiking and camping / by Paul Mason.
       p. cm. — (Recreational sports)
    Includes index.
    ISBN 978-1-59920-129-0
    1. Hiking—Juvenile literature. 2. Camping—Juvenile literature. I. Title.

    GV199.52.M37 2007
    796.5—dc22

                                                    2007004593

Edited by Vanessa Lanaway
Text and cover design by Pier Vido
Page layout by Pier Vido
Photo research by Naomi Parker
Illustrations by Boris Silvestri
Map on pp. 28–9 by Pier Vido

Printed in U.S.

Acknowledgements
The author and the publisher are grateful to the following for permission to reproduce
copyright material:

Front cover photograph: Hikers on Otter Trail, South Africa, courtesy of ABPL/Lanz Von Horsten/
Photolibrary.

Photos courtesy of:
Anne Ackermann/Getty Images, p. 15; Brian Bailey/Getty Images, p. 18;
Peter Cade/Getty Images, p. 4; Ron Chapple/Getty images, p. 26; Ian Cumming/Getty images,
p. 27 (bottom); Blasius Erlinger/Getty Images, p. 11 (top); Stuart Fox/Getty Images, p. 20; Derek
Lebowski/Getty Images, p. 14; Mike Powell/Getty Images, p. 30; Mike Timo/Getty Images, p. 19;
David Trood/Getty Images, p. 24; Yellow Dog Productions/Getty Images, p. 21; Andres Balcazar/
Istockphoto, p. 12; Norman Chan/Istockphoto, p. 27 (top); Peggy Easterly/Istockphoto, p. 16;
Paige Falk/Istockphoto, p. 22 (top); Jim Mercure/Istockphoto, p. 5; Jillian Pond/Istockphoto, p.
10; Matthew Ragen/Istockphoto, p. 22 (bottom); David Rose/Istockphoto, p. 11 (bottom); Aviad
Se/Istockphoto, p. 7; Dragan Trifunovic/Istockphoto, p. 27 (middle); ABPL/Lanz Von Horsten/
Photolibrary, pp. 1, 6; Dennis Welsh/Photolibrary, p. 9; Photos.com, p. 8.

While every care has been taken to trace and acknowledge copyright, the publisher tenders
their apologies for any accidental infringement where copyright has proved untraceable.
Where the attempt has been unsuccessful, the publisher welcomes information that would
redress the situation.

Please note
At the time of printing, the Internet addresses appearing in this book were correct. However,
because of the dynamic nature of the Internet, we cannot guarantee that all Web addresses will
remain correct.

Contents

Glossary words

When a word is printed in **bold**, you can look up its meaning in the glossary on page 31.

Recreational sports

Recreational sports are activities we do in our spare time. These are sports that people do for fun, not necessarily for competition.

You have probably tried some recreational sports. Maybe you would like to know more about them or to find out about new ones? Try as many as you can—not just hiking. Also try biking, fishing, kayaking, climbing, and snorkeling. This will help you to find one you really love to do.

Benefits of sports

Recreational sports are lots of fun, but they also have other benefits. People who exercise regularly usually have better health. They find it easier to concentrate and do better in school or at work.

"Of all exercises, walking is the best"
U.S. President Thomas Jefferson in a 1786 letter.

Hiking and camping

If you want to get outside, what about going for a hike? After all, walking is free, and you do not need any special training! You could hike in your local area, on a guided city tour, or on a country trail.

Sleeping under the stars

Many people combine hiking with camping under the stars. There are plenty of places to try camping. You might start in your own backyard, where all you will need is a tent. You might not even need a tent on a warm night.

WATCH OUT!

The outdoors can be a dangerous place. Make sure you are able to keep warm at night, find a shelter, and find food, in case something goes wrong.

Getting started

Most people's first hike lasts a day or less. All you need for a day hike are comfortable shoes and clothes, water, and an idea of where you want to go.

"Take a two-mile walk every morning before breakfast."

U.S. President Harry S. Truman on his 80th birthday, giving advice on how to live to be 80.

Places to hike

There are plenty of different places to go for a day hike. Here are a few ideas.

Your local area

Follow a new route around your local area. Take your time and look around. You might see things you have never seen before.

A trail through your city

Lots of cities now have special walking trails. They are designed to show you interesting places.

Out of town

National parks and other country areas have great trails. These can be long or short. Short trails might take an hour to finish. Long trails can take several weeks..

Even if you only have a morning or afternoon free, it is possible to hike through some spectacular scenery.

Hiking tips

There are a few rules most hikers follow when planning a walk:

- Plan your time carefully. It is better to finish your walk early than to have to walk back in the dark.
- Take someone who knows the way. Some people do their first hikes with an organized group, to be sure they make it home on time.
- Take enough to eat and drink. Hiking uses a lot of energy
- Check the weather forecast. The weather can change quickly.

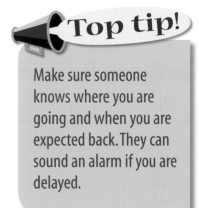

Top tip!

Make sure someone knows where you are going and when you are expected back. They can sound an alarm if you are delayed.

Having enough water with you is very important.

Hiking Equipment

You don't need special equipment for a day's hiking. Just wear comfortable shoes and clothes.

Shoes and boots

For short walks, the most important thing is to have shoes that will not make your feet sore. If the route might be slippery, shoes with good grip will be useful.

On longer walks, many hikers wear special walking boots. These have stiffer soles, are usually waterproof, and are more comfortable for long hikes than ordinary shoes.

Specialist hiking boots are designed to be safe and comfortable for long hikes.

"If you want to forget all your other troubles, wear tight shoes."
The Houghton Line, November 1965

Clothing

Most hikers wear clothes that are fairly loose. Unless the weather is cold, shorts are best for hiking. Even if it rains, the skin on your legs will dry more quickly than long pants would.

For longer hikes, some people wear special clothing. This keeps them from getting too sweaty, and makes sure they do not get too hot or cold.

What to take

It is always a good idea to take these things on a hike:

- backpack
- warm top
- water
- cell phone, if you have one
- snack, such as a banana
- waterproof top, if it looks like it might rain

In hot, sunny weather, you should also take:

- sunscreen
- hat to block the sun

In cold weather, you might bring:

- warm hat
- gloves

Top tip!

Avoid wearing clothes with a **seam** that rubs underneath your backpack straps.

The right equipment will make your hike more enjoyable.

backpack

hat

warm top

lightweight, waterproof top

gloves

9

Planning your route

When planning your route, it is a good idea to find out as much about it as you can. For example, planning a good place to sit down and eat your lunch will make your hike more fun.

Planning questions

Here are some things to think about when planning a hike:

- How long will it take to get to and from the start of the trail? Remember to include this in your plans.
- Are you hiking for exercise or to look at scenery and animals along the way?
- Will you be walking quickly or slowly?
- What kind of ground does your route cover? Flat ground is much easier, but hilly ground is often more interesting.

Planning a route with rest stops at viewpoints such as this makes a hike much more fun.

Judging distance

It will be easier to plan your hike if you know how far you can walk in a set time. If you think you have enough time to cover 6 miles (5 km), remember that you have to get back, too. Make sure that your destination is no more than 3 miles (5 km) away.

"Anywhere is walking distance, if you've got the time."

U.S. writer and actor Stephen Wright.

Naismith's Rule

Naismith's Rule helps hikers to plan how long a walk will take them. To calculate the time, assume that an average hiker will cover 3 miles (5 km) in an hour. Add an extra half hour for every 980 feet (299 m) of steep climbing, up or down. Take off 10 minutes for every 980 feet (299 m) of gentle downhill. Make sure you allow at least this much time to complete your hike before it gets dark. Younger hikers should expect to cover only about three-fourths of this distance, so will need to reduce their distance by 25 percent.

Check the weather to avoid hiking in hot sun, where there is no shade.

You can walk farther and faster in cool weather!

Finding your way

The best hiking trip can turn into a nightmare if you get lost. Finding your way is a crucial hiking skill.

Marked trails

Marked trails are walks with signs showing you which way to go. This type of trail is easy to follow, which is great for beginner hikers.

On marked trails, the signs often tell you the destination, how far you have to go, and how long it will take to get there. Remember that not everyone walks at the same speed. You might be faster or slower than the signs suggest.

Ready-made, marked trails can sometimes be followed by people who use a wheelchair.

Top tip!

Use a map to plan a shorter way home, in case the hike takes longer than expected.

Using a map

Maps are useful for hiking, even if you are on a marked trail. Maps are covered with tips about where your hike is taking you. Use these clues to plan your day on the trail.

To figure out how fast you will be able to walk, study the slopes and the type of ground you will be walking over. Watch for any high points on your route. They might be good places to stop and enjoy the view. A map will also show you any forests. In hot weather, plan to spend the hottest part of the day walking through these shady areas.

Contour lines

Contour lines are lines on a map that show how steep a slope is. If they are close together, the slope is very steep. If they are far apart, the slope is not steep.

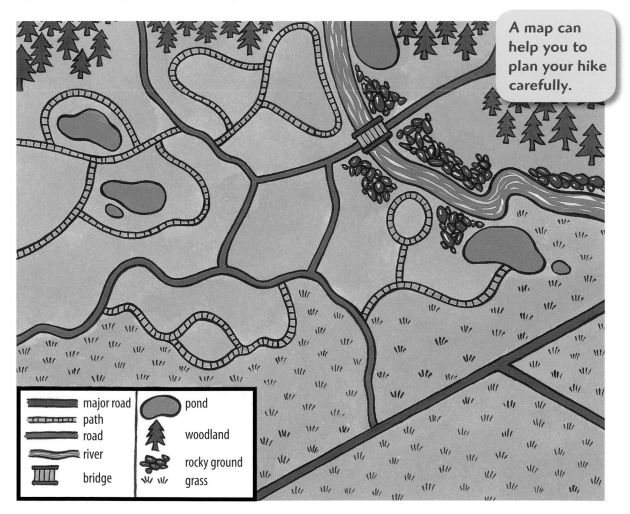

A map can help you to plan your hike carefully.

major road
path
road
river
bridge
pond
woodland
rocky ground
grass

13

Overnight trips

Some hikes take several days. You will need to carry a tent, a sleeping bag, and cooking gear on these longer hikes.

Kinds of tent

A small tent is light and easy to carry while hiking. Tents can be divided into parts, such as poles, **flysheet**, and **inner tent**, for carrying. This means you can split the weight between the people who will be sleeping in the tent.

Nylon tents are lighter than **canvas** ones, especially if they get wet. A nylon tent is best for carrying with you on a hike.

"Backpacking is the art of knowing what not to take."

Sheridan Anderson in "Baron Von Mabel's Backpacking."

The best thing about a dome tent is that it can be easily moved.

Where to camp

Many people start camping in their own backyard. They can practice putting their tent together and make sure all the poles and **pegs** are there. Best of all, it is not far to walk for breakfast in the morning.

Other people hike to **campsites**. Some campsites have showers, toilets, and a cooking area. Some even have swimming pools or tennis courts.

Marked trails sometimes have special camping areas. These are shown on trail maps, and are often free to use. They usually do not have any **facilities**, except perhaps a toilet.

Top tip!

Always be sure camping is allowed before pitching your tent.

A good sleeping bag will keep you warm and comfortable.

Pitching your tent

Pitching your tent in the wrong place can give you an uncomfortable night's sleep. Choose your **pitch** with care.

Choosing a place

When deciding where to put your tent, there are certain things to look for and things to avoid.

Look for . . .	Avoid . . .
Level ground	Sloping ground
Grassy or soft ground	Rocky or hard ground
Shade from sun or rain	Exposed areas
Higher, dryer ground	Low-lying, damp areas

Once you have found a good place, lie down where you plan to put your tent. This is a great way to check if the spot you have chosen feels comfortable.

A level, shady spot like this is a great place to put up your tent.

WATCH OUT!

Never camp in a dry riverbed. If it rains, you could be swept away by the sudden rush of water in a flash flood.

> *"Take only photos and leave only footprints."*
> Old hikers' saying, meaning that hikers should leave thing how
> they found them, without damaging their surroundings.

Pitching a dome tent

Follow these tips to make sure you have the best chance of a good night's sleep.

1 Check the site for anything that could damage the floor of the tent or disturb your sleep, such as rocks or ants' nests. If possible, remove them.

2 Lay out your inner tent, spreading out the tent floor. Peg down one corner so that it cannot blow away.

3 Put the poles together carefully. Letting them snap together can damage them. Slide the poles through the sleeves of the tent.

4 Attach one end of each pole to the tent floor.

5 Push the poles gently through, then attach the other ends.

6 Peg down the floor.

7 Put the flysheet in place.

8 Attach the flysheet and peg open the flysheet door.

Eating and cooking

You do not need to take much food on a day hike. However, you will need extra food and cooking gear for overnight trips.

Day hikes

Good food for day hikes includes cereal bars, fruit, dried fruit, and bread and cheese. These are light to carry, and will give you energy throughout the day. Some people also carry chocolate. This is good for emergencies, because it can give you a quick burst of energy.

It is important to drink plenty of water while on a hike.

Water

Water is crucial for human survival. You could live for weeks without food, but only a few days without water. Having water with you and knowing where you can get more is very important.

Overnight trips

On overnight trips, most people enjoy a hot meal at the end of the day. This means they carry cooking gear with them. Special camping stoves are small and light, so they are easy to carry. Lightweight cooking pans are also useful.

Technique

Cook a lightweight camping meal

The best food for an overnight hiking trip is light to carry and gives you plenty of energy. Dried foods such as pasta are ideal.

Ingredients
- pasta (about 2 cups per person)
- salt
- jar of pesto
- thinly sliced cheese

1 Cook the pasta with salt in a pot of boiling water.
2 Drain off the water, then put the pasta to one side.
3 Fry the pesto in a new pot, then add the pasta.
4 Stir in the cheese.
5 Serve to your smiling, hungry friends.

Top tip!

Always be careful cooking outdoors, because fire spreads very quickly.

Cooking and eating together after a long day's hike is great fun.

19

Survival skills

With careful planning, hiking and camping are very safe. Even so, unexpected events can happen. The weather could change, or you might get lost. It is important to know what to do if something goes wrong.

Surviving heat

Extremely hot weather is very dangerous for humans. Without food, water, and shelter, extreme heat can be deadly.

Water

Water is especially important for survival in hot conditions. Make sure you take plenty of water with you on a hike. If you run out, here are some tips that might help you to find more.

- Animals and birds usually head for water at dawn and dusk. Following their route should take you to water.
- Digging behind the dunes on beaches sometimes produces **brackish** fresh water. Once water starts to appear, stop digging. The deeper water will probably be saltier.

Carrying plenty of water is always important. In dry conditions it is crucial.

Losing body water

Your body uses water all the time, especially when it is hot. This is because it sweats in order to stay cool. If you are trapped in hot conditions, try to make sure your body loses as little water as possible.

Technique

Conserving body water

These tips will help you to keep your body from losing water.

1 Wear clothes that keep your skin covered.
2 Stay cool. Do not lie on hot ground or run around.
3 Stay out of the sun. Try to rest in the shade, if possible.
4 Talk as little as possible and breathe through your nose.
5 Do not drink seawater or alcohol, as they will make you more dehydrated.

WATCH OUT!
Be very careful collecting water anywhere that alligators could be lurking.

Stay in the shade to conserve body water.

Waterproof clothes will help keep you dry, which means you will also stay warmer.

Sweep snow off your tent to keep it from collapsing.

Surviving cold

Extreme cold is as deadly for humans as extreme heat. Your body uses energy trying to stay warm. It starts to shiver and shake uncontrollably. If you stay very cold for a long time, you could die.

Cold and wet

Cold and wet conditions are especially dangerous. Body heat is lost more quickly through wet clothes than dry ones. Your body uses up its reserves of energy much faster than usual.

Conserving body heat

These tips will help you to stay safe in cold conditions:

- keep as warm as possible, ideally in some kind of shelter
- stay dry, again using some kind of shelter if possible
- to save energy, only move around if you have to
- eat and drink as regularly as possible

Top tip!

Always have a hat in your bag. Putting on a hat is one of the best ways to conserve body heat.

Build a cold-weather shelter

This is a simple shelter that almost anyone can build quickly.
All you need is a plastic sheet and a line. Small shelters are
easiest to keep warm, so keep the shelter as small as possible.

1 Find a sheltered spot, and string a line between two trees.

2 Lean brush against the line, making a tunnel. This will give insulation for warmth.

3 Throw the plastic sheet over the brush, then pin down the edges with rocks (or use sticks as pegs).

4 Add more brush inside to lie on.

5 Block off the ends with more brush.

Starting a fire

Starting a fire is an important survival skill. But it must be done carefully, especially in dry conditions. Be very careful so that your fire does not spread.

Even in a hot country, you sometimes need a fire to keep you warm at night.

Building a fire

To build a fire, you need four things:
- waterproof matches
- kindling, which must be very thin and dry. Twists of dry grass, feathers, a shredded bandage, or cotton from a t-shirt are all good kindling.
- larger kindling, such as thicker dried grass and twigs
- fuel, such as larger pieces of dry wood

1 Use a match to light the kindling.

2 Once the kindling is glowing, gently blow on it. Add it to the middle of the larger kindling. Keep blowing! The kindling should light up.

3 Once the kindling is lit, add smaller pieces of fuel in a teepee shape.

4 Once these are burning, add larger pieces of fuel.

Navigation

If you get lost, navigation, or finding your direction, is an important skill. Ideally you should be carrying a compass or even a **GPS device**. Without one of these, you will need to find another way to figure out which direction you should go.

Finding north and south

This is a simple way of finding out roughly which direction is north and which is south. Begin about an hour before noon.

1 Push a short stick—about 12 inches (30 cm) long—into the ground, pointing straight up in the air.

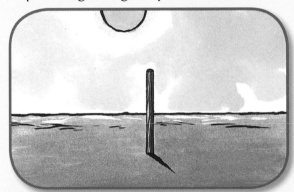

2 Every ten minutes, put a small pebble or some other marker at the tip of the stick's shadow.

3 Keep doing this until you start placing the pebbles further away from the stick.

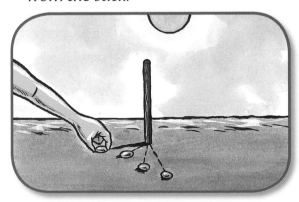

4 The line from the base of the stick to the closest pebble shows you roughly where north and south are. In the Northern Hemisphere, north is at the pebble end. In the Southern Hemisphere, north is at the stick end.

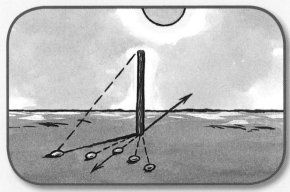

Fit to hike

There is nothing worse than running out of energy on a hike. Your legs become wobbly and every step is hard work. Fortunately, doing some exercise can help.

Exercise for hikers

The best exercise for hikers is simply to walk more. Think about the trips you make by car or bus every day. Some might be trips you could do on foot, such as walking to school.

On longer journeys, you could ride a bicycle instead of walking. Cycling builds up your leg muscles, which is great for hiking.

Swimming is also good training for hikers. If you want to work your legs extra hard, grab a kickboard, and swim for a few laps using only your legs.

Any walking you do will be good practice for your next hiking trip.

Weight

Hiking is less tiring if you carry less weight. This could be less weight in your pack, or less weight on your body! Try not to eat fattening food such as fries, burgers, soda pop, candy, or ice cream. Eating these foods once in a while is fine, but not every day.

Fitness plan

This weekly plan will help you get fit enough to race along the trail, ready to grab the best camping spot!

Saturday	Hike to a campsite with your family. Set up tents.
Sunday	Pack up and hike home.
Monday (and the rest of the week)	Rest day (except for walking to and from school).
Tuesday	Go for a swim, use a kickboard for 20 minutes.
Wednesday	Rest day (apart from walking to and from school).
Thursday	Go on a bicycle ride with a friend.
Friday	Rest day.

Hiking to isolated places such as this can be a tough job, so it pays to be as fit as possible.

Hiking and camping around the world

These are some of the world's most famous hiking trails. Some of them take days or even weeks to complete. People come from far and wide to walk these routes.

Highest mountain

Name   Circuit of Mont Blanc
Location   France, Italy, Switzerland
Length   93 miles (150 km)
This hike goes around Mont Blanc, the highest mountain in Europe. It visits three different countries.

Picturesque hiking

Name   GR20
Location   Corsica, France
Length   112 miles (180 km)
The GR20 follows the mountainous spine of Corsica, an island off the French coast.

Ancient trade routes

Name   Annapurna Circuit
Location   Himalayan Mountains
Length   186 miles (300 km)
A trek following ancient trade routes between Nepal and Tibet.

Pilgrims' trail

Name   Way of St. James
Location   Northern Spain
Length   466 miles (750 km) from Roncesvalles to Santiago. An ancient trail taken by pilgrims. They travel to see the grave of St. James at Santiago de Compostela.

World's highest trail

Name   Mt. Kilimanjaro
Location   Tanzania, Kenya
Altitude   3.66 miles (5.89 km)
The highest hiking route in the world! Although it is hard work, this route takes hikers to the top of Africa's highest mountain.

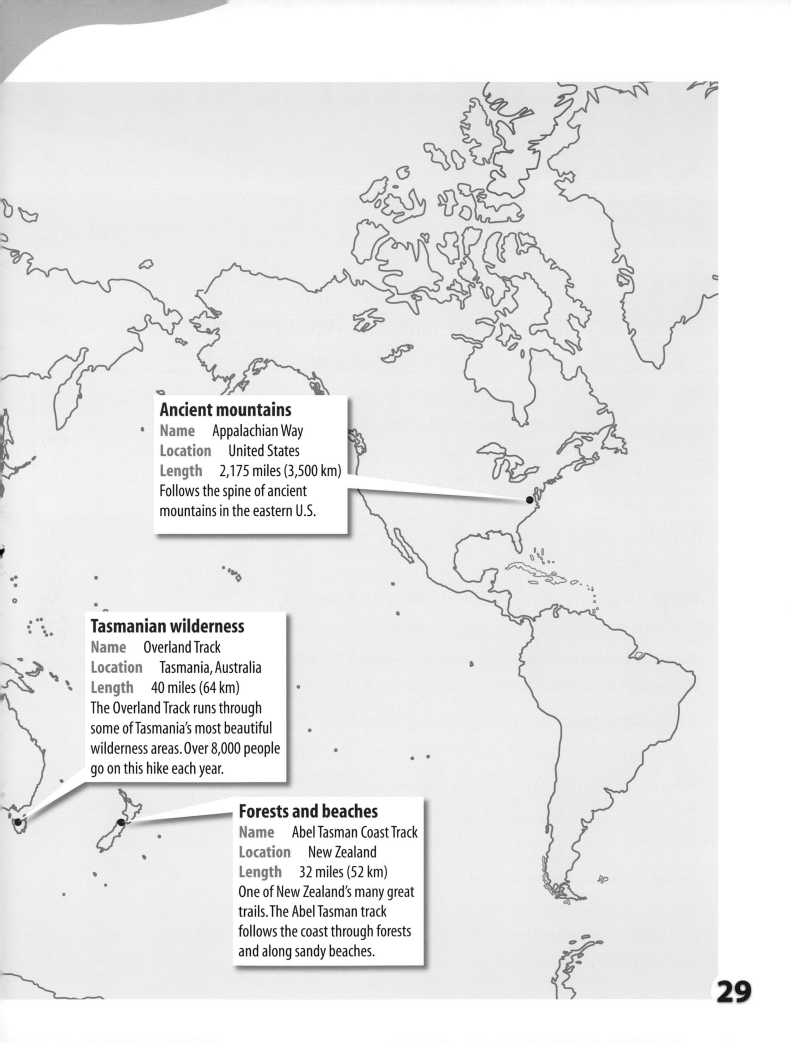

Ancient mountains
Name   Appalachian Way
Location   United States
Length   2,175 miles (3,500 km)
Follows the spine of ancient
mountains in the eastern U.S.

Tasmanian wilderness
Name   Overland Track
Location   Tasmania, Australia
Length   40 miles (64 km)
The Overland Track runs through
some of Tasmania's most beautiful
wilderness areas. Over 8,000 people
go on this hike each year.

Forests and beaches
Name   Abel Tasman Coast Track
Location   New Zealand
Length   32 miles (52 km)
One of New Zealand's many great
trails. The Abel Tasman track
follows the coast through forests
and along sandy beaches.

Interview: Camping crazy!

Andrew has been camping since he was a baby, and hiking since he could walk. He has traveled around the world with a tent and backpack.

How did you first start hiking?

My parents used to take me, my brother, and my sisters away on camping trips all the time. They had an old van that they used to load us all up in for the weekends. Sometimes we'd just stay near the van, other times we'd hike to a deserted beach somewhere.

What do you most enjoy about hiking and camping?

Oh, the fact that you can just go anywhere you like and find somewhere to put your tent. You don't have to depend on anyone else, no one bothers you, it's really cheap, and you're in the fresh air.

What is the best campsite you have been to?

I can't tell you, because then everyone will go there!

What was your worst camping experience?

Everyone's tents blowing down during a storm in India, a day's hike from anywhere. Then we realized we didn't have a repair kit.

What is your favorite hiking book?

Annapurna 8000m by Maurice Herzog. It's really about the first expedition ever to climb Annapurna, but the description of the hike to the mountain is amazing.

Glossary

brackish

salty

campsites

places where camping is allowed; campsites often have things such as toilets, showers, and even a shop or restaurant

canvas

heavy fabric made out of cotton

facilities

things that are designed to be helpful to campers, such as toilets, showers, and places to dry wet clothes

flysheet

the outer skin of a tent, which shelters it from rain

GPS device

Global Positioning System, an electronic device that can tell you exactly where you are

inner tent

the inner part of the tent, including the floor and an inside lining to the tent's "skin"

pegs

lightweight metal sticks with a curved end, used to attach a tent to the ground

pitch

the spot where you put your tent

seam

a line of stitching that joins two pieces of fabric together

Index